About the author

Jeff is an aluminous of Olkejuado High School and the Technical University of Kenya. When not writing he enjoys reading, travelling, listening to music and dancing. *The Life of Koko* is his first book of poetry to be published.

This is a work of fiction. Names, characters, businesses, places, events and incidents are either the products of the author's imagination or used in a fictitious manner. Any resemblance to actual persons, living or dead, or actual events is purely coincidental.

THE LIFE OF KOKO

JEFF KENIOTA

THE LIFE OF KOKO

Vanguard Press

VANGUARD PAPERBACK

© Copyright 2022
Jeff Keniota

The right of Jeff Keniota to be identified as author of this work has been asserted by him in accordance with the Copyright, Designs and Patents Act 1988.

All Rights Reserved

No reproduction, copy or transmission of this publication may be made without written permission.
No paragraph of this publication may be reproduced, copied or transmitted save with the written permission of the publisher, or in accordance with the provisions of the Copyright Act 1956 (as amended).

Any person who commits any unauthorised act in relation to this publication may be liable to criminal prosecution and civil claims for damages.

A CIP catalogue record for this title is available from the British Library.

ISBN 978 1 80016 245 7

*Vanguard Press is an imprint of
Pegasus Elliot MacKenzie Publishers Ltd.*
www.pegasuspublishers.com

First Published in 2022

**Vanguard Press
Sheraton House Castle Park
Cambridge England**

Printed & Bound in Great Britain

Dedication

This book is dedicated to Alice Matata

When you grow up

You will look back

And see the footprints

Of the long journey

Inside the Life of Koko

Acknowledgements

To Pia, you came in like an angel and touched me when I was giving up. My friends, Stefano, Davide and Daisy, I thank you very much for the encouragement. Finally, to Fred Amunga, the special one.

Book One
Highlights

Village at the turning corner
panoramic view with great honour
great Mount Elgon blue in the morning
head up and tail end so warming
sunrise so sweet and promising
love and life harnessing

Iconic tall trees for reference
shape and height create the difference
'turn left after the eucalyptus on the right'
traveller arrives even at night

Houses inside the homesteads
round and high like rocket heads
smooth decorated mud walls
thatch crafted to guide rainfalls

Blue smoke filters through thatch
eagles round up chicks for catch
man yawns under cool mango tree
toilworn woman works extra for free
careful under soot on smoked fish
shortly air full yummy dish

Thirsty sheep bleats under midday sun
tethered goat entangled tries to run
as hunter's dogs sprint past
impala ahead is fast

Winds bring in delicious
smell of brown sugar so precious
like burning sweet potatoes
sugar stones keep economy on toes
canes from farm run the jaggery
brown sugar makes liquor for toggery.

In the evening men attach to long straws
from communal pot for draws
of brown porridge brew so warm
tales keep the group in swarm
empty pockets entertain sponsor
in return pot overflows for the boozer

"Heard latest scandal around?
Juma went out of bound
was stopped by girl's scream
rescuer said t'was shameful at the stream
on ladies' bath shelter both naked
victim terrified when man invaded"
never happened such news
wait for the elders' views

Emerge host and his wife
both women married to share life
happy in traditional union
not partaking church communion
but enjoying love of children
akin to normal brethren.

Lady-man eats gizzard
symbol of power in family blizzard
children call her father
even those of her brother
she is man to brother's wife
with equal respect in life

Children showered with love
everyone defends them all above

Nanzala the man
Nanzala the woman

Cheeky villagers
Prefer imageries
Nanzala the bull
Nanzala the winker

Nanzala with the ball
Nanzala the bearded bull

For clarity they are known
female father been thrown
childlessness was considered crime
returned home to regain prime
family took her back
inheritance she didn't lack

Starts up new life
as man and found wife
imagination no one stretches
not important such stresses
life is happiness
evil is quirkiness

Village DJ on turntable
playing rhumba for the able
villagers to shake and twist
waist and wrist
first slowly to rhythm
one-two step in rhyme
then fast and freestyle
cut and repeat in a while
for angle they shout
for a retake of the bout

Night marathons for rustlers and runners
naked possessed wading off evil earners
both nuisance to peaceful sleep
once caught the runner begs a steep
blood spirit must remain shush

Night spirit is powerful
run naked through night
no one got courage to fight
an old man once caught
stuck naked woman who taught
Christian religion at school
night spirit in full
'girl what you do here?'
teacher trembles in fear

Nights are long
fear and song

Villagers bang doors
spirit of the lake roars
nyavava they call
like whirlwind they roll
spirits escorted with noise to lake
no one knows where they originate
they're danger to children
bring death and migraine

Dogs bark
in the dark

Book II
The Life of Koko

Sweet sixteen sends her packing
exodus of teens marking
new beginning
no bargaining
brother and three sisters
no hiding like gangsters
all to marriage
first love courage
strangers at night
to respect in daylight
new home in mystery
to write history

First she hides face
shy for accepting chase
fiancé and Koko in love
tells mother above
word reaches father
daughter "kidnapped" not farther
report to calm family about girl
negotiate dowry and stop the whirl
cow and goat for Koko
girl so dark as cocoa

New life welcoming
prince charming
inside lion cage all time
no school bell to chime
honeymoon so perfect
no snitching prefect

swap saliva
swap life

Téte-â-téte fable
smooth rhumba on turntable
great dancer
village bouncer

Clan is Nakatekoko
herdsman calls her Koko
erases other names too
only for her boo

Honeymoon over
long days hover
baby moon over
pregnancy rover
Christmas over
new life mover

wrong tribe
can't subscribe
sure impregnated
not integrated
man solaces in liquor
loses job and gets weaker

Long nights alone
crickets chirping along
someone working his hand
not music from a band
scary sound at ventilation
shortly arrives husband in jubilation

Koko now a doormat
can't afford doughnut
joins village whisperers
violence and portent murderers
slaps and whips not forbidden
cries 'd alert small children

Not for better but for worse
she stands with remorse
he raids mother's kitchen
she loses even the kitten
sleeps on stomach so empty
enter bugs and lice so steady
symbol and epitome of poverty
torment those without property

Beautiful dark
scary black
become moot
as soot

Ugly
Poor
Rags
Filthy

Ah! loss of mama Maria
another vacuum after no career
Koko opts for family chemistry
not most appreciated industry
pays bills and hot plate
buys pen and book for school
uniform and Sunday wool

Hubby in accident with torn toe
mother says no, better try tomato
exit man enter son so awesome
child to labour quite cumbersome
their sweat man pinches
responds with punches

Man disappears
mother's order it appears
better him around mad and thief
than nowhere even if chief
police destroy illegal distillery
charge Koko on African traditional diary
pays fine from savings and family fundraiser
tap dries on funds organiser
children linger at school gates
world on shoulders as money abates

Man in place not far
kind to women for small bar
children need food
unaware of after mood
sister don't worry our secret
man helps women no regret
along created sect
evil mission to infect
disease to spread
women seeking bread

Children exam paid from money
not much to afford more honey
headache and fever
pain and weakness forever

Motherhen bothersome and invasive
must be told not persuasive
why you talk alone, asks sister-in-law
your mother, replies Koko below
village radio carries stigma
AIDS has arrived like magma

Koko rudely condemned
rain comes so damned
roof leaks like Thompson Falls
water sips into mud walls
slimming disease attacks forth and back
happy virus have walk in park
no medicine no diet may be deity
full wrath of family and society

Village goss and a sneer,
hanging on for end so near
on mat every day is a decade
villagers bet in banana arcade

Her body in jactation
dear mama for lactation
she cries
she tries

Sight white as sheet
thin head to feet
bony with blanket skin
hairless head as chin
clothes fall down
no food from town

I was a fool
'Twas not cool
I suffer for my stupidity
people full of rigidity
cries won't righten
actions were rotten
woman must suffer
no sympathy offer

Tired hubby threatens with push
to throw her in bush
skinny not a hyena can salivate
wishes without life so private
no more teardrops from her eyes
dry eyelids won't rise

In bed carers debate and watch
her linen to throw or wash
their hands are fired
their spirits are tired
not dying
no buying

Soap
food
medicine

Donor funded people
expose her in triple
screaming buckets, t-shirts and food
villagers passing by for wood
stand to whisper of home infested
Koko no more interested
cruel publicity
not simplicity

For her ears hear
afar and near
footsteps and breath
mood and wreath

Waiting son for long
biting teeth strong
saying no word
none to the guard

Boy is here her joy
feels her like broken toy
heart beats double
her life in rubble

The end is not near
The end is here

Adios!

Book III
The queen of nightmare

This woman is a woo man,
came in second but can't hear non
rebels and sways husband
off they form a band
in new land so far to rule
desires are plentiful

This woman is a woo man
they call her Big Mum
power and influence at finger
builds and crushes to linger
dreams are radio heard by all
wishes are orders overall

This woman is a woo man
enhanced, diminished and wan
researches medicine and people
crowns and names steeple
blesses and curses with power
hires and fires all over

This woman is a woo man
hubby wants another woman
woman brings sister
can't stand a monster
man wants yet another
her cousin to become a mother

This woman is a woo man
rules every human
takes lion's share
doesn't care
to queen they all bow
favour they must wow

This woman is a woo man
cousin becomes real woman
from womb a daughter
Big Mama kidnaps after
cousin is too childish
but for nine month-ish

This woman is a woo man
way to market a boy ran
to meet her for female is omen
can't risk an empty oven
black jack seed on occipital
ward off evil in the capital

This woman is a woo man
speaks to living and dead human
the old woman came in my dream
so clear I saw her seam
tell 'em to move from my house
her orders arouse

This woman is a woo man
with the order of a Roman
fertile land abandoned too
like law of zoo
harvests where she never sow
drives family low

This woman is a woo man
preys on chicken and ban
sorry never knew was yours
worry not everything is ours
mama please
afford me lease

This woman is a woo man
other people wan
mere wing to Koko
take leg to the loco
stolen chicken shared
best parts spared

This woman is a woo man
another comes with can
begs for food and oil
anything to boil
all in hands of queen
in control so keen

This woman is a woo man
Sunday's top layman
humblest effigy for Eucharist
before priest from Bucharest
white dress and pink headgear
white robe purple scurf spit fear

This woman is a woo man
back home focus greed marksman
lend me that will give back
All poor has goes to dark
Later take this to poor
That way debt is paid for sure

This woman
is a woo man

Book IV
Hounded at birth

It's a boy
bundle of joy
doctor calls Alloys
young girl says Royce
mother-in-law says Pig
because boy is big
insult of a name
at birth for excuse so lame
hatred and revenge it seems
why name someone to doom

Duty for father is first offence
farmer through the fence
Piglet you come for the piglet?
Yes with anger and tear droplet.
On way through bush
Man emerges after a push
Ha! Carrying your brother?
Asks without bother
Animal responds with snout
Boy pulls back snot

Snout
Snot
Snout
Snot

Koko sees son; why you cry?
Comprehend the pain with no reply
Papa picks animal piglet from son Piglet
Snout runs to a sack of millet
Snot to herd goats goes
Calm and happy with what he does

Monday boy rises for school
At door blood drips in pool
Mother and father side by side
Boy hesitates to go inside
Stones in hand for mother
Stick in hand for other

Boy goes to kitchen for water
It isn't any hotter
Ten shillings on foot path
Picks money and does math
Gives to mother after beef
Why they call me thief
She says
He prays

Boy needs a book
Oh what a look
Shorts are torn
Like gored by horn
Go well my boy
You are my joy

In class girl shouts
Others come out
On his head lice
Big as white rice
Boy goes under desk in shame
Nail tears his shorts in frame

Car backlights they say
They laugh to keep him at bay
White buttocks exposed
Vulnerable for canes imposed

Boy is bright in class
Eyes clear like glass
Loves books but has less
Reads upside down for less
Roast cob for boy from borough
For a book to borrow

Last high marks in review
Earned him precious chicken stew
Big Mama said give him head
Part for stupid read
Chicken is chicken he ate
Scored higher than the top mate

Book V
Tribute

Man who was older than his own father

There was a man called Fanta
A friend to my father
The only man older
Than his own father
He had grey hair
His father had none nor bald
His mother was even older

Oh Fanta
man who holds a dialogue
Talking with himself
He with himself
To ward off the village muggers
Until one day
The boys discover him
And give a chase
Though old Fanta runs
For his dear life and money

Fanta was a name he got
Because he staggered
Just after one shot
He could not stand a Fanta

And Fanta one day
Fell into a pit latrine
He was drunk as usual
He spent three days inside
The hole
A passerby hears a faint voice
The worms had started
Feasting on Fanta
But he was alive

On his wedding day
He slept with shoes
He had gone long without shoes

Fanta had nine lives
And we thought he was immortal
Until he died and disappeared
His born was taken by mistake
The search began
He was found and brought home
Fanta you lived well

Simple Kayai

The last wife of the doctor
With wearing beads
On her slim waist
Young and striking beauty
Age of the man's firstborn
Entrepreneurial
Peanut business
Toiling in the farm
To feed her children
Sardines are her favourite
Occasionally smoked tilapia
plenty of vegetables

Black tea without sugar
Occasional sweet potato
Or lemon grass
Or brown sugar
Cracked feet from toil
Rags
They call her Mama Kayai

That drunk gardener

Hornbill, Agip, Box
They called you hoax
From dawn you rose
To till and break the land
Bananas, cassava, maize
All crops you cured
At dusk you staggered back
From taking your daily shot
Speaking to yourself

Those who work don't eat
Those who eat don't work eat
Was your slogan

You went to the dairy office
To collect milk money
Anthony and his brother
Ambushed you and snatched
All the money
Before you could reach home
When you reported to their mother
They beat you up
A trained soldier and his brother
Beating up an old man
Save for their sister Grace
That tiny girl
Who yelled at her brother
And whipped him to stop
She was a no-nonsense lady
Full of shame the soldier
Retuned to the barracks

One day comes arrogant John
Another relative
So full of himself
Picks up a drunken fight
In the evening you
Were the punching bag
In the morning you
Were the beast of the farm

By the way we revenged for you
We had gone to harvest honey
The bees had hidden the honey
Inside a living tree
We couldn't cut it
Disappointed we saw John coming
Drunk on his way home
We hid behind the long grass
And scared him
He ran, removed his white shirt
We used another route home
Found him narrating his ordeal
Armed thugs he said
So funny his side of story
We laughed and laughed

John went away

The pen you supplied me
Pen for my school
Pen for my soul
Pen to sign my future
That pen is why I honour you
You armed me with a pen
I lay on the mat floor
near the warm fireplace
and you in your reed bed.
you narrated to me bedtime stories
you were rich in African oral narratives
every night you told a new fable
And whenever I asked for a repeat

You never hesitated
The hare and the tortoise
The crocodile and the hare
The squirrel and the farmer

The hare and the leopard

The day your female namesake came
that night you asked me
to relocate from the kitchen we slept in
When she came, Nekesa
I had to peep and find out
I couldn't see
I heard
You teaching her to make your bed
T'is this way
Not that way

I knew Nekesa
Notoriously Nekesa of the testicle
I didn't know why
But she was classy
She carried a filter less cigarette
On her ear, like a carpenter's pen
And smoked it
with burning side inside her mouth

Your soap
No one touched it
Because your rubbed it
In your ass
Ha ha
Did I miss a point
You feared snakes
You had this one shirt
You wore Monday to Monday
January to December
Only changing it for a new one
At Christmas

This is my song for you

Erneo the bachelor

There came a man
Who bought a tiny piece of land
And settled with his three sons
A teenager who was never there
And small boys
They herded cattle and goats
For a meal
Sometimes survived on cassava
Or grasshoppers and guavas
You were the point of reference
Of poverty and property
Once caught in a neighbour's granary
Trying to scoop some grain
Your trousers were full of patches
Of different colours and materials
But your sons were my playmates

Punch

At breakfast rich children
Take milk thickened tea with buttered bread
Their chicken eat leftovers
From last evening's dinner table
The poor drink sugarless
Milk-less tea
Occasionally brown sugar
Rarely left over from previous dinner

Relative Figure

That my father has brothers
And sisters
That my mother has brothers
And sisters
His siblings are his equals
Regardless of gender
They are all my fathers
I call the females my aunts
But still they are father figures
Mother calls them all mulamwa
She is their wife
Their children are my brothers
And sisters
Our child, our children, ours
Mother's sisters are my mothers
A trail of them
Mother's brothers
Are my uncles
Their children are my cousins

Christmas in the shire

It's merry Christmas
Avoid Matayos centre
They eat bananas for Christmas
Stay at Tangakona village
They eat chapatti for breakfast
Mandazi for breakfast
Chicken and rice for dinner
Rice and beans for lunch
Soda and barbecue
They wear new clothes
They wear new shoes
They chew gum and
Display white teeth

The town centre is full of teenagers
Taking photos in makeshift studios
Happy people
The houses are plastered with fresh dung
And colourful mud from the swamp
With flowers and Merry Christmas message
Children are allowed to taste beer
On knees a deep sip from the straws
The warm beer is light but fills the stomach
The wines and spirits are for the adults
Strong to knock down those who abuse

Anointed son of a woman

You were famous in photos
Grandma said you were out
Meaning you were far away
You were a Christmas tourist
Bringing pears
And cooking yummy mandazi
And you left
when you came to settle
Village life was tough
You got a village girl
You got booze and weed
All for the need

You started to hammer in me
What you thought to be discipline
Daily doses of bitter words and strokes
Like a jealous kid
You said I ate your mum's food
Asked me where was mine

My moment came
As you struck your woman
Your mum with sharp torch
On her endowed behind
And there your struck
With your cane
She cried aloud
I laughed
Came her turn
She grabbed your balls
And stepped on you
Till you couldn't breathe
The domestic show
She held post match reviews
To the villagers to know
That she was the new boss

With her wish you revenged on me
For not doing this and that
Your woman was my classmate
Big among girls
With my aunt
She grabbed a boy
And stepped on him
He dropped out of school
And she followed suit
She spoke like a radio
Moving information
From source to destination
In details without fear
She blew like wind

Now she was my mama
Commanding respect
Demanding it
I found it weird
I couldn't be wired
I defied and rebelled
You came tough and open
Said I was doomed
I refused to lose
From your family herds boy
Hey uncle I still rise

The soldier

Tall dark and handsome
A friend of my father
Came with a new radio cassette
We danced to rumba
Came with rifle oil
healed our skin diseases
cuts, burns and wounds
smoked military cigarettes
drunk beer from bottle

Called me frog
Because I had big eyes
Called mother mudfish
Because she was too black
You sent Ruth to stay with mudfish
She stayed

The Good old Margherita

Granny Nerima Margherita
Tall and beautiful
With a pipe
Puffing and blowing
With a long walking stick
Longest distance
To get tobacco from Ochola
Remember that day
When you gave us dried meat
But turned out to be full of worms

And remember the story
Amoro the village girl
And Namafura the ogre
When she helped the beast
He designed a tattoo
She went away with his smell
Was to be a secret
Finally due to pressure
She revealed
And the ogre was angry
He came to attack the village
To eat Amoro
But was speared to death
And all those he had swallowed
Were recovered
Only the old lady
Who kept forgetting
Her items was remained
In the stomach of the giant

I was out herding goats
I heard women crying
You had just left
My father blew the horn
To relay message
He also took a bicycle
And went to inform far relatives
The biggest funeral
I saw your sons
The good, the bad the ugly
John drinking inguli
Rolling in the dust
Sleeping in the bush
Your daughters, Sister Monica
And Aquinatta, mourning you
Like a state funeral in the micro nation
You were the queen
They came from wide and far
Clansmen and friends
Neighbours and government
To say goodbye
Feasts laid down
To celebrate your life
Long sweet life

Most high Grand dude

Come rain come sunshine
You wore mud gumboots
You always woke up at five
Switched on your radio
And waited for station to open
One of the two radios in the village
Your left after morning tea
Pushing your bicycle
Thumping the gumboots
In darkness to the market place
To the clinic, Doctor
Family Planning Association
Yet you had more than thirty
Children and five wives
And swarm of grandchildren

In the evening you brought
Bread and sugar to second wife
Or was it the new first wife
Sugar to third, now second
And sugar to fourth now third
The fifth or fourth was a concubine
The first was forgotten
But you stood tall
Every Tuesday and Saturday grandsons
With a basket to get beef
For their grannies
Sometimes the grannies appeared
All of them at the clinic
For a day out shopping

You wore nice sandals
Exposing childhood scars
Of jigger infested toes
Which told your African story
Of a long journey
Travelled to current status
Of a clinician, a village doctor
In the evening I recounted
To you my day
About your goats, sheep and calves
We surveyed your land
I trailed you as you inspected
With a big club across your shoulders
I answered questions
Always justifying
Why queen should have the best
Even when I was wrong
In return a reward of peanuts
From your third or fourth wife
You had many

Oh BOW bull of western
On this day I had to struggle
With strong calves
And lock them inside their shed
To prevent them from suckling
After i washed my hands
You called me aside
Gave me sweet mandazi
And praised me before queen

The other day Patrick
Queen's brother damaged your radio
You were so angry
you never missed the news
on the BBC and KBC
You picked up the radio
And returned to town
You left all shaking

Finally the day you said goodbye
I remember once again
Just you and I in a room
In a hospital
You struggling to breathe
While I waited
For what I don't know
Just waiting for you to finish
And either return to life or die
There was no way back

I watched you cough
and breathe your last
It was an expiry
Living for ninety-six years
Called for celebration not mourning
We threw a party
Grandsons carried your coffin
From one house to another
For men don't die
Your spirit had to visit your wives
At one point cheeky ones played tricks
They released the coffin
Making it heavy for two people
We thought you did not want to go
We thought you hated the woman

Thereafter we danced
We ate and drunk
We gave thanks
For a life well lived doctor.
Thank you Grand-dude

Book VI
Song for Papa

There is a big wide gap
From your last grasp
Because you never said goodbye
You never let me pass by
To see you and accept
That you were not exempt
That one day you'd die
That idea that I couldn't buy
It was impossible for you
From my point of view
That you will go too soon
That you will go to the moon

Let me take myself back
You stood by the rack
Spreading my books to dry
So that I won't have to cry
Without them to school
Mother sat by on the stool

Like many memories there was young love
Many problems but it shown above
When the record player was there
You played music everywhere
At home I was your assistant
As long as I was resistant
To scratch the disc head
I didn't have to go to bed
Until it was late enough for the kids
As a reward I danced and sipped from the reeds
The warm brown beer from the large pot
Endless supply of water to keep it hot

The day of the accident
Was the end of the advent
I had my heel entangled in the spokes
You brought the bike down stokes
And home you safely took me
And let me be

The craftsman
The Deejay
The carpenter
The mason
The family rep

There is nothing you didn't know
That day you took a cigar to gnaw
You had hardly puffed
But you quickly stuffed
It inside your pocket
Because your father came like a rocket

He spoke while it burned
Only when turned
To leave did you slap thigh
And toss the cigar butt high
You ran to the house for water
To cool the burning matter

When you cut your toe
With a machete like a foe
Granny came with gun oil
It burned the wound like a hot coil
It was funny for a laugh
In response you had a face so rough

Still on memory lane
There was no wind vane
But in January the wind
Blew from hind
We set up the oxen
To have the soil broken
For planting season
With no reason
I spat out a dirty word
You laughed as a reward
"Victoria, flex your ass"
I had called out to pass

Then you set in to drink
Often on the brink
You twice slept outside in the dew
Mother couldn't carry you in due
Then you failed to get off bike
And fell off like a spike

There were ups and downs
In villages and towns
To get this and that
You wore your hat
Mother had great start-up
Before your work break-up
Good lotions for her dark skin
Biscuits for my morning spin
Sweets that turned my teeth brown
But you kept us under the crown

With no town job the village was tough
No coin in the pocket without a trough
Mother was into moonshine
You were out from dawn to nine
You brought a tilapia when lucky
And war when things were mucky

You tried farm hand and other jobs
Fixing houses and ferrying cobs
Then that thief lured you with money
You had your hand trapped in the honey
The police came looking for you
The law wanted you to hew
You left mother in limbo
Villagers with hands akimbo
Police raided her illegal distillery
And took away her machinery

Mother had tried selling sardines and paraffin
They sold but less than a muffin
Your brothers woke up late
Mother without a mate
Things were thick
Mother was sick

I couldn't forgive us
when I was thinking of focus
You sneaked away without goodbye
Because I was not nearby
You went too soon
Even before it was noon

I will never say Adios!

www.ingramcontent.com/pod-product-compliance
Lightning Source LLC
LaVergne TN
LVHW091552060526
838200LV00036B/800